THE COMMON LAW LIBRARY

McGREGOR
ON
DAMAGES

First Supplement
to the
Nineteenth Edition

Up-to-date to October 2015

BY

JAMES EDELMAN

Justice of the Federal Court of Australia

AND

HARVEY McGREGOR

CBE, Q.C., D.C.L., S.J.D.

CHAPTER ON THE HUMAN RIGHTS ACT
CONTRIBUTED BY MARTIN SPENCER Q.C.

CHAPTERS ON PROCEDURE
REVISED BY JULIAN PICTON Q.C.

SWEET & MAXWELL  THOMSON REUTERS

Published in 2015 by Thomson Reuters (Professional) UK Limited
trading as Sweet & Maxwell,
Friars House, 160 Blackfriars Road, London, SE1 8EZ
(Registered in England & Wales, Company No 1679046.
Registered Office and address for service:
2nd floor, 1 Mark Square, Leonard Street, London EC2A 4EG)

For further information on our products and services, visit:
http://www.sweetandmaxwell.co.uk
Typeset by Wright and Round Ltd., Gloucestershire
Printed and bound in Great Britain by CPI Group (UK) Ltd, Croydon, CR0 4YY

No natural forests were destroyed to make this product;
only farmed timber was used and re-planted.

British Library Cataloguing in Publication Data

A CIP catalogue record for this book
is available from the British Library

ISBN 978–0–41405–315–1

HOW TO USE THIS SUPPLEMENT

This is the First Supplement to the Nineteenth Edition of *McGregor on Damages*, and has been compiled according to the structure of the main volume.

At the beginning of each chapter of this Supplement is an abbreviated table of contents from the main volume. Where a heading in this table of contents has been marked by the symbol ■, this indicates that there is relevant information in the Supplement to which the reader should refer.

Within each chapter, updating information is referenced to the relevant paragraph in the main volume.

ACKNOWLEDGEMENT

In 1961, Harvey McGregor produced the 12th edition of what was then known as *Mayne and McGregor on Damages*. Many developments had occurred in the law of damages during the quarter century since the previous edition. Consequently, there was a great deal more of McGregor's work in the 12th edition than there was from Mayne. Harvey was so much more than just an exceptional lawyer. But he became known worldwide for his fine legal acumen. Over the next 54 years *McGregor on Damages* became the work for which Harvey rightly received acclaim as the world's leading authority on damages.

In late October 2014, Harvey contacted me to ask if I would consider taking over *McGregor on Damages* after the 20th edition. I had rejected the same enquiry, years earlier, when it was made through a mutual acquaintance. But times had changed and my academic commitments had nearly vanished. Harvey wanted the book to be written by a single author. He said, and I agree, that "the great merit of the book is that its vast substance is written by a single person so that all the parts dovetail". Harvey was also in excellent health. Both he and I thought that this would mean a handover some time in 2019. That was not to be. Unfortunately, on 27 June 2015, Harvey passed away. Characteristically, he had been working on this supplement until very shortly before his death.

Although my association with Harvey was very brief, it has been an honour to be able to complete this supplement and to continue Harvey's *magnum opus*. One story suffices here to describe Harvey's deep learning, his characteristic generosity, and his kindness. In July 2000, I had just completed a draft of my doctorate on gain-based damages. In that month, the House of Lords delivered its decision in *Attorney General v Blake* [2001] 1 AC 268. That decision lead to much revision and rewriting. I had been immersed in the decision for several months when Harvey came to Oxford to speak on damages issues, including on the *Blake* decision. The room at New College was packed to the rafters. Harvey was very critical of *Blake*. In my thesis, however, I lauded it. At the conclusion of his presentation I asked a series of questions designed to defend the decision. Harvey responded softly and politely explaining that damages and compensation were synonyms. The latter was not a species of the former. His answer was steeped in the learning of half a century's work on damages. None of his answer changed anything in my doctorate. My work was much the poorer for not understanding the nuances in his answer. Harvey's speech, his answers to my

[v]

questions 15 years ago, and his subsequent writing, were a strong factor in my understanding of the error in my thinking that a party who deliberately breaches a contract should, without more, often have to disgorge profits. The context of *Blake* was fundamentally important, in particular Lord Nicholls' much neglected comment that George Blake's undertaking, was either a fiduciary obligation or was closely akin to one. Much may therefore depend upon the relationship between contractual and fiduciary obligations. As a great scholar, Harvey's work was also constantly moving. His doubts about the *Blake* decision became more muted. By the 19th edition of *McGregor on Damages* the scare quotes had been removed from the phrase restitutionary damages. Chapter 14 now contains, in part, a defence of gain-based damages, although one which plays close attention to the factual circumstances of various categories of case. And, on the issue of whether it matters to have a characterisation of obligations as either contractual (common law) or fiduciary (equity), the 19th edition now begins with the sentence: "Damages are now defined in this book quite simply as an award in money for a civil wrong."

I will write more about Harvey in the preface to the 20th edition of *McGregor on Damages*, which will also commence with an acknowledgement from one of his learned colleagues. Nevertheless, it was necessary for me to begin this first supplement with these introductory words to acknowledge the debt that I, like all others in the legal profession, owe to Harvey. My debt will only be repaid in part by an attempt to maintain the quality and integrity of the work, which should always remain as *McGregor on Damages*.

JAMES EDELMAN
October 2015

CONTENTS

BOOK FOUR
PARTICULAR CONTRACTS AND TORTS

TABLE OF CASES

TABLE OF STATUTES

INTRODUCTION

Insert a new paragraph after para.1–016:

It must, however, be acknowledged that this position is becoming increasingly **1–016A** difficult to maintain. The observations of Lord Browne-Wilkinson in *Target Holdings v Redferns*, quoted in the paragraph above, if applied as an absolute proposition would not be consistent with those of Lord Toulson in *AIB Group (UK) Plc v Mark Redler & Co Solicitors* [2014] UKSC 58; [2014] 3 WLR 1367 at [59], who observed that in *Bank of New Zealand v New Zealand Guardian Trust Co Ltd* [1999] 1 NZLR 664 Tipping J had "rightly observed that while historically the law has tended to place emphasis on the legal characterisation of the relationship between the parties in delineating the remedies available for breach of an obligation, the nature of the duty which has been breached can often be more important, when considering issues of causation and remoteness, than the classification or historical source of the obligation".

BOOK ONE

COMPENSATORY DAMAGES

BOOK ONE

PART TWO

THE HEADS OF COMPENSATORY DAMAGES

NON-PECUNIARY LOSSES

5–003 NOTE 4: Add at the end of the note: Since these procedural reasons are irrelevant to cases heard in the Employment Tribunal, His Honour Judge Serota held in *De Souza v Vinci Construction UK Ltd* March 2015 EAT, not following two earlier decisions by which he was not bound, that the *Simmons v Castle* 10 per cent uplift has no application in the Employment Tribunal.

5–007 NOTE 18: Insert before the last sentence of the note: And the Supreme Court in *Rhodes v OPO (by his litigation friend BHM)* [2015] UKSC 32, reversing the Court of Appeal, held that *Wilkinson v Downton* did not apply in relation to the publication of an autobiographical book by a father which might lead to his child's psychiatric illness.

5–012 Insert a new note before "the mental anxiety" on the last line but two of the paragraph:

NOTE 40a: *Rothwell* has been statutorily reversed in both Scotland and Northern Ireland, each enacting that asbestos-related pleural plaques shall constitute an actionable personal injury: see, respectively, Damages (Asbestos-related Conditions) (Scotland) Act 2009 and Damages (Asbestos-related Conditions) Act (Northern Ireland) 2011. *McCauley v Harland & Wolff Plc* [2014] NIQB 91 is a Northern Ireland damages case following upon the statutory reversal.

Insert a new paragraph after para.5–014:

5–014A An interesting extension beyond injury to feelings has been proposed, and put into effect, by Mann J in the class action entitled *Gulati v MGN Ltd* [2015]

EWHC 1482 Ch. The eight claimants sued for invasion of their privacy which came about by the hacking of their phones by journalists who listened to their voicemails on a daily basis over several years and then reported on what they heard in very many articles addressed to the public. Mann J thought it was wrong to confine the damages to compensation for distress and injured feelings; there should be compensation for the invasion of privacy per se, representing damages for loss of personal autonomy, loss of dignity, loss of standing in the community. People who had very significant parts of their private lives exposed and then reported on over a prolonged period were entitled to significant compensation, and large sums were awarded (see in particular [168]–[169], [702], and on the awards themselves see para.45–008A, below). What the Court of Appeal will make of this extension to the coverage of damages for non-pecuniary loss, which has good sense behind it, remains to be seen.

5–016   NOTE 63: Add at the end of the note: Since these procedural reasons are irrelevant to cases heard in the Employment Tribunal, His Honour Judge Serota held in *De Souza v Vinci Construction UK Ltd* March 2015 EAT, not following two earlier decisions by which he was not bound, that the *Simmons v Castle* 10 per cent uplift has no application in the Employment Tribunal.

BOOK ONE

PART THREE

THE LIMITS OF COMPENSATORY DAMAGES

CHAPTER 7

REDUCTION OF DAMAGES FOR CONTRIBUTORY NEGLIGENCE

Insert a new paragraph after para.7–006:

That the decision on apportionment is so much a matter of impression is **7–006A** dramatically illustrated by *Jackson v Murray* [2015] UKSC 5, a case from Scotland of a child running into the path of an oncoming vehicle, a not unfamiliar story in the annals of contributory negligence. Not only was the trial judge's reduction of the 13-year-old girl's damages by 90 per cent changed down by the Scots appeal court to 70 per cent and further changed down by the Supreme Court to 50 per cent but also the reduction by the Supreme Court was only by a bare majority, the minority agreeing with the Scots appeal court's 70 per cent. Reference was made to the potentially dangerous nature of driving a car, which could do much more damage to a person than a person was likely to do to a car. And it was agreed that an appeal court could only interfere with an apportionment made if it could be said that it lay outside the generous ambit within which reasonable disagreement was possible. Clearly, however, different views were taken as to whether here this generous ambit had or had not been crossed. The majority speech and the minority one are both worth perusal. This guidance of the Supreme Court Justices in *Jackson* on the correct approach of an appellate court to apportionment in contributory negligence has since been adopted by the Court of Appeal in *McCracken v Smith* [2015] EWCA Civ. 380, where there had been a collision between a minibus and a trial bike being recklessly and illegally driven. It was again held, though here unanimously, that the generous ambit within which reasonable disagreement was possible had been crossed, and the court increased, rather than reduced, the trial judge's 30 per cent attributed to the claimant, the bike's pillion rider, to 50 per cent (together with an agreed 15 per cent on account of the claimant's not wearing a crash helmet).

NOTE 22: Add at the end of the note: In *Blackmore v Department of* **7–007** *Communities and Local Government* Unreported 23 October 2014 County Court, where the cause of an employee's injury and subsequent death was by the combined effect of his smoking and his exposure to asbestos by his employers, the trial judge held that he need not base the deduction for contributory negligence on a mathematical calculation of relative contribution to risk. Instead he considered that the employers should bear the lion's share of responsibility on account of their prolonged breaches of statutory duty and, while the risk from the employee's smoking was probably twice or thrice the risk from the employers' asbestos, he assessed the contributory negligence at 30 per cent.

CHAPTER 8

REMOTENESS OF DAMAGE

8–019   Insert a new note at the end of the paragraph:

NOTE 54a: It was held in *Heneghan v Manchester Dry Docks Ltd* [2014] EWHC 4190 QB that *Fairchild*, together with the related *Barker v Corus*, applied as much to the contraction of lung cancer as to the contraction of mesothelioma. See the case at para.10–021 n.84a, below.

8–024   Insert a new note after the first sentence of the paragraph:

NOTE 74a: For a different approach to consecutive injuries, see *Reaney v University Hospital of North Staffordshire NHS Trust* [2014] EWHC 3016 QB at para.8–090 n.448, below.

8–063   NOTE 298: Add at the end of the note: *McCracken v Smith* [2015] EWCA Civ. 380 (at para.7–006A, above) is a further case where *ex turpi causa* and contributory negligence are intertwined.

8–090   NOTE 448: Add at the end of the note: The claimant in *Reaney v University Hospital of North Staffordshire NHS Trust* [2014] EWHC 3016 QB contracted a disease causing damage to her spinal cord leading to semi-paralysis. When in hospital the defendant's negligence caused her to sustain pressure sores and associated disabilities, which exacerbated her condition and made a significant difference to her physical wellbeing and her care needs. Foskett J, after a full review of the authorities, saw the case as a reflection of the principle that a wrongdoer must take his victim as he finds him and, if that involves making the victim's damaged condition at the time of the wrong worse, full compensation for that worsened condition must be made: *ibid.* at [70]. Accordingly, the claimant was entitled to damages based upon the condition in which she found herself in the wake of the defendant's negligence. A series of well-known cases of high authority concerning two consecutive personal injuries (*Baker v Willoughby* [1970] A.C. 467; *Steel v Joy* [2004] 1 W.L.R. 3002 CA) and two consecutive incidents of damage to goods (*Performance Cars v Abraham* [1962] 1 Q.B. 33 CA; *Carslogie S.S.Co v Royal Norwegian Government* [1952] A.C. 292) were distinguished.

8–134   Add at the end of the paragraph: From exposure to platinum salts in their employment, the five claimants in *Greenway v Johnson Matthey Plc* [2014] EWHC 3957 QB developed sensitivity to platinum. While this sensitisation did not produce physical or physiological harm to them, it prevented their continuing in their work involving contact with platinum. It was held, applying SAAMCO, that the scope of the employer's statutory duty lay in the safeguarding of its employees from the risk of personal harm and the claimants were therefore debarred from suing for their economic loss: see *ibid.* at [34].

Insert a new note at the end of the paragraph: **8–147**

NOTE 746a: The Court of Appeal in *Stacey v Autosleeper Group Ltd* [2014] EWCA Civ. 1551 relied on both the *Girocentrale* and the *Borealis* cases to hold that the buyer of a motor home was entitled to damages for breach of warranty for his loss, by way of costs of litigation with his sub-buyer, as his failure to notice the inconsistency between the gross weight stamped on the chassis plate and the greater gross weight warranted was not reckless.

NOTE 781: Add at the end of the note: The liability of the employer in **8–156** *Greenway v Johnson Matthey Plc* [2014] EWHC 3957 QB, considered at para.8– 134, above, was in breach of contract as well as in tort for breach of statutory duty. The result was the same. The employer's duty, operating through an implied term imposed by the law, was to maintain a safe place of work and to care for the physical safety of employees; thus the implied term was exactly co-extensive with the tortious obligation. So in contract as in tort the scope of the duty did not go beyond physical injury to reach economic loss: see *ibid.* at [43]–[47].

Insert a new note at the end of the first sentence: **8–177**

NOTE 859a: A further case in which *The Achilleas* and the assumption of responsibility test was held to have no application is *Saipol SA v Inerco Trade SA* [2014] EWHC 2211 (Comm) where there was a sale of sunflower seed oil contaminated in the shipping of it: see *ibid.* at [15]–[18]. Also in *SC Confectia SA v Miss Mania Wholesale Ltd* [2014] EWCA Civ. 1484, where there was a sale of defective garments, the Court of Appeal held *The Achilleas* to have no possible application: see *ibid.* at [15], [24]–[26].

CHAPTER 9

MITIGATION OF DAMAGE

Insert a new paragraph after para.9–006:

In *Thai Airways International Public Co Ltd v KI Holdings Co Ltd* [2015] **9–006A**
EWHC 1250 (Comm), Thai Airways claimed damages from KI Holdings for
breaches of contract in relation to the supply of economy class aircraft seats.
Some seats were delivered late and others were not delivered. Thai Airways was
prevented from using five of its aircraft for 18 months pending the delivery of the
seats from another supplicr. The issue at trial was whether Thai Airways had
mitigated its loss. Leggatt J endorsed these three different rules for mitigation

(see [32]), although suggesting that the three rules had an underlying unity based on causation. With respect, the underlying unity does not lie in the notion of causation but, as Leggatt J recognised at [33], the unity lies in a rule that damages are assessed as if the claimant acted reasonably, if in fact it did not act reasonably: quoting A. Dyson and A. Kramer, "There is No 'Breach Date Rule'" (2014) 130 LQR 259 at 263.

The discussion in the paragraphs that follow is consistent with the observation by Leggatt J that the concept of acting reasonably can be deconstructed into various norms of reasonable conduct including the dominant norm that it is reasonable for a claimant to enter an available market as soon as possible to obtain a substitute for a defendant's performance.

9–017   Add at the end of the paragraph: The point was recently reiterated by Lord Toulson (with whom Lord Neuberger, Lord Mance and Lord Clarke agreed) in *Bunge SA v Nidera BV* [2015] UKSC 43 at [81]:

> "the so-called duty to mitigate is not a duty in the sense that the innocent party owes an obligation to the guilty party to do so (*Darbishire v Warran* [1963] 1 WLR 1067, 1075, per Pearson LJ)."

9–018   NOTE 40: Add at the end of the note: See also *Bunge SA v Nidera BV* [2015] UKSC 43 at [81] per Lord Toulson.

Insert new paragraphs after para.9–030:

9–030A   *White and Carter v McGregor* [1962] A.C. 413 (discussed at para.9–023, above) has made a further appearance in *MSC Mediterranean Shipping Co SA v Cottonex Anstalt* [2015] EWHC 283 (Comm), this time not to be applied. The Swiss seller of a large consignment of raw cotton to a purchaser in Bangladesh, both being companies, contracted to have it shipped by a carrier in 35 of the carrier's sea containers. The contract of carriage provided that for 14 days after the discharge of the cargo in the containers the shipper was entitled to retain the containers without charge, after which time what is today referred to as container demurrage (see para.15–073, below) at a specified daily rate until the containers were returned, a provision that was completely open-ended so that payment of demurrage could continue indefinitely.

9–030B   The market for raw cotton having collapsed shortly after the conclusion of the contract of sale, the purchasing company sought to extricate itself from the contract and did not collect the cotton that remained in the containers up to the time of the trial. The purchaser attempted not to make payment to the seller but its attempt, by resort to litigation, failed and payment was eventually made. On payment, title passed out of the seller who then had no control over the containers still with the cotton in them.

Leggatt J, after a careful analysis of the facts and the law, held that there had been a repudiatory breach of the contract of carriage once it became impossible for the seller to procure collection of the goods and the delay in collecting them had become so long as to frustrate the commercial purpose of the venture. The carrier was claiming more and more demurrage payments as the days went by, so had not accepted the repudiatory breach, and the *White and Carter* case would suggest that the carrier was entitled to continue with the contract in this way. **9–030C**

Accepting that the carrier had to show a legitimate interest in keeping the contract alive, Leggatt J examined the legitimate interest principle in the wider context of the need for good faith in contractual dealings, a requirement he considered was now coming to be recognised in the common law. He came to the conclusion that there was no legitimate interest to decline to accept the repudiatory breach since after a certain date the carrier was suffering no loss and was keeping the contract alive merely in order to claim demurrage indefinitely: see the whole discussion from *ibid.* at [94] onwards. **9–030D**

Had Leggatt J held that the carrier had an unfettered right, as he put it, to decline to accept the repudiatory breach, he would have held the container demurrage provision to constitute a penalty. For this aspect of the case, see paras 15–030A to C, below. **9–030E**

NOTE 172: Add at the end of the note: In *SC Confectia SA v Miss Mania Wholesale Ltd* [2014] EWCA Civ. 1484 there was a sale of defective garments which the buyer sold on and, on discovery of the defects, wished to retrieve the garments from its sub-buyer but could not do so as the sub-buyer had gone into liquidation. The Court of Appeal held that there was no failure to mitigate, but the one reasoned judgement is not thought to be too clear either on mitigation or, for the purpose of damages, on the correct valuation of the garments. **9–044**

Insert a new paragraph after para.9–135:

In *Fulton Shipping Inc of Panama v Globalia Business Travel SAU* [2014] 2 Lloyd's Rep. 230 Popplewell J held that a shipowner claiming damages for charterers' repudiation of a time charter need not give credit for the capital value of having sold the ship on repudiation for a greater sum than the value of the ship at the contractual date for redelivery under the charter. This is clearly correct, being an illustration of, in the above words of Robert Goff J in *The Elena d'Amico*, a decision independent of the contractual breach made on the claimant's assessment of the market, amounting to a crystallisation of the loss. Popplewell J indeed makes this point, and with a reference to *The Elena d'Amico*, but his judgment follows the approach of placing heavy reliance on causation to come to the conclusion on mitigation. **9–135A**

CHAPTER 10

CERTAINTY OF DAMAGE

NOTE 26: Add at the end of the note: *Armory v Delamirie* (1722) 1 Strange   **10–006**
505 was brought into play in a very different context by Mann J in *Gulati v MGN
Ltd* [2015] EWHC 1482 Ch, a case of serious and prolonged phone hacking (the
case is dealt with at para.5–014A, above and para.45–008A, below). Where the
details and extent of the phone hacking that was in the defendant's knowledge
were not provided or even destroyed, Mann J was prepared to arrive at conclu-
sions in favour of the claimants within, as he put it, the bounds of reality: see [85]
et seq. and [218].

Insert a new note after the first sentence of the paragraph: **10–012**

NOTE 39a: In assessing the uncertain loss of profits arising from a supplier's
breach of an exclusive supply agreement in *Globe Motors Inc v TRW Lucas
Varity Electric Steering Ltd* [2015] EWHC 553 (Comm), the judge had little

alternative, after very lengthy submissions by both sides on the calculation of the damages, to taking a broad brush approach.

10–013   NOTE 44: Add at the end of the note: The application of the reflective loss principle in relation to damages is further discussed in the factual context of *Malhotra v Malhotra* [2014] EWHC 113 (Comm) at [53]–[63], *Energenics Holdings Pte Ltd v Ronendra Nath Hazarika* [2014] EWHC 1845 Ch at [60]–[70], and *Barnett v Creggy* [2014] EWHC 3080 Ch at [92]–[99].

10–021   Insert a new note at the end of the paragraph:

NOTE 84a: *Heneghan v Manchester Dry Docks Ltd* [2014] EWHC 4190 QB was a claim brought on account of the death from lung cancer of a smoker who had been exposed to asbestos during his working life. The defendants were six of his employers over a period of some 10 years; earlier employers were not sued. It was agreed between the parties that the share of the deceased's exposure to asbestos attributable to the six employers sued was some 35 per cent; also agreed was the distribution of the exposures between the six. It was agreed by the medical experts that on the balance of probabilities it was the exposure to asbestos and not the smoking that caused the death. The issue to be decided was whether the defendants were each liable for the whole of the damage caused or for only the 35 per cent. In a long complex judgment, Jay J decided for the 35 per cent, applying the *Fairchild* principle together with the apportionment ruling in *Barker v Corus*.

In contrast, Jay J refused to award damages in *Saunderson v Sonae Industria (UK) Ltd* [2015] EWHC 2264 QB. In that case, group litigation was brought by thousands of claimants for personal injuries arising from negligence and public nuisance when fire broke out at the defendant's chemical plant in Kirkby. The plant was near the claimants' homes or workplaces. The claimants failed to establish liability. At [186], Jay J explained that the *Fairchild* principle meant that it was incumbent on the claimants to prove on the balance of probabilities that they were within the relevant envelope of material risk as that concept is properly understood. It is insufficient that there was a risk in the sense that the claimants had *some* exposure such as a minuscule exposure, measurable only in parts per trillion. The exposure must be at a level that was capable of causing personal injury.

10–083   Insert a new note after the penultimate sentence of the paragraph:

NOTE 348a: Also in *Tait v Gloucestershire Hospitals NHS Foundation Trust* [2015] EWHC 848 QB the *Langford* method is adopted: *ibid.* at [88].

10–089   NOTE 381: Add at the end of the note: , where *Hayes v South East Coast Ambulance Service NHS Foundation Trust* [2015] EWHC 18 QB is cited as a case in which the chance of reconciliation was very high.

NOTE 494: Add at the end of the note: Cases appearing in this section on **10–111** certainty of loss dependent on the defendant's actions—*Lavarack, Horkulak* and *Durham Tees*—come under consideration in *IBM United Kingdom Holdings Ltd v Dalgleish* [2015] EWHC 389 Ch. See the case at para.31–031 n.185a, below.

Insert a new paragraph after para.10–119:

The Golden Victory [2007] 2 A.C. 353 has of late been much in evidence, on **10–120** account of contracting parties arguing for the assessment of the damages at a time after the date of breach of contract because of the future realisation of contingencies.

Some cases have concerned breach of warranty where shares in a company have been sold; in all of the cases the argument has failed. The issue received consideration by Popplewell J in the earliest case, *Ageas (UK) Ltd v Kwik-Fit (GB) Ltd* [2014] EWHC 2178 QB. The breach of warranty resulted from an overstatement in the company accounts of revenue and assets by reason of the bad debts of the company at the time of contracting being understated. By the time of trial four years later the bad debts had become much less. The level of bad debt was the future uncertain contingency, which later became certain, upon which the party in breach relied to reduce, if not eliminate, the damages. Popplewell J rightly held that *The Golden Victory* was not in point. The measure of damages fell to be assessed in the usual way at the time that the contract was made which was also the time of breach. The risk of what would happen to the bad debt position was effectively transferred to the buyer who was entitled to the benefit if the company business did well and be subject to the loss if it did badly. The compensatory principle was unoffended and there was no windfall to the buyer: see the discussion from *ibid.* at [29]. Similar is *Hut Group Ltd v Nobahar-Cookson* [2014] EWHC 3842 QB. Neither the assets and liabilities nor the profit and loss of the company had been fairly presented and the question was, once again and with *The Golden Victory* again in mind, the extent to which matters following the breach of warranty could be taken into account in the assessment of the damages. Blair J, who not unreasonably was unclear as to what the future uncertain contingency here comprised, held that such matters were not to be taken into account as, again, the outcome of all contingencies were risks trans-ferred to the buyer which reaped the benefit or suffered the loss depending on how the business did: see the discussion at [212]–[219]. As for the curious case of *Bir Holdings Ltd v Mehta* [2014] EWHC 3903 Ch, where the claim was by the seller of shares on account of its breach of warranty entitling the buyer to retain a substantial part of the purchase price and where *The Golden Victory* was again brought into play, matters following upon the breach were not taken into account in the assessment of damages, although it appears that the case did not involve future uncertain contingencies: see the discussion from [66]–[81].

The issue arose again in the Supreme Court in *Bunge SA v Nidera BV* [2015] UKSC 43. In that case, unlike Hamblen J whose decision is discussed above at para.10–118, the Supreme Court confronted the question of whether *The Golden Victory* should be applied, and whether it was correctly decided. The sellers argued that it was necessary to take account of events occurring after the breach which showed that the same loss would have been suffered even without the repudiation. The buyers' first argument was that, consistently with the view expressed at para.10–118, the majority view in the *Golden Victory* should not apply to a single cargo. The second argument for the buyers was that *The Golden Victory* was wrongly decided. The third argument was that the agreed damages clause had excluded the compensatory principle enunciated in *The Golden Victory*.

As to the first argument, Lord Sumption (with whom Lords Neuberger, Mance and Clarke agreed) said that the dicta from Lord Scott of Foscote in *The Golden Victory* should not be understood as confining the principle to cases involving situations involving successive performances. The principle also applied to cases involving a single instance of performance. Cases involving a single instance of performance might be factually different but the compensatory principle applies to them in the same way. Lord Toulson, who also agreed with Lord Sumption, said that there was "no logical foundation" for a distinction between a single instance of performance and successive performances (at [87]).

As to the second argument, Lord Sumption held that the decision in *The Golden Victory* was neither new nor heterodox. His Lordship rejected the clarion call for certainty on the basis that, although important, "it can rarely be thought to justify an award of substantial damages to someone who has not suffered any" (at [23]). Lord Toulson, who also agreed with Lord Sumption, also expressed the view that *The Golden Victory* was correctly decided and consistent with previous case law (at [87]).

As to the third argument, Lord Sumption held that agreed damages clauses were not necessarily to be regarded as a code, and further that there was no presumption that an agreed damages clause was intended to exclude the common law. However, such a damages clause may be assumed, in the absence of clear words, not to have been intended to operate arbitrarily. An arbitrary operation would include on which produced a result unrelated to anything which, by the compensatory principle, the parties could reasonably have expected to approximate to the true loss. In this case, the agreed damages clause was not a complete code and the provision was consistent with the application of the compensatory principle.

At [21], Lord Sumption said:

"The real difference between the majority and the minority turned on the question what was being valued for the purpose assessing damages. The majority were valuing the chartered service that would actually have been performed if the charterparty had not been wrongfully brought to a premature end. On that footing, the notional substitute contract, whenever it was made and at whatever market rate, would have made no difference because it would have been subject to the same war clause as the original contract ... The minority on the other hand considered that one should value not the chartered service which would actually have been performed, but the charterparty itself, assessed at the time that it was terminated, by reference to the terms of a notional substitute concluded as soon as possible after the termination of the original. That would vary, not according to the actual outcome, but according to the outcomes which were perceived as possible or probable at the time that the notional substitute contract was made. The possibility or probability of war would then be factored into the price agreed in the substitute contract."

A similar observation about the basis for the minority decision (concerned with valuing the *contract* itself) was also made by Lord Toulson at [88].

BOOK TWO

NON-COMPENSATORY DAMAGES

CHAPTER 12

NOMINAL DAMAGES

NOTE 8: Insert at the end of the cases listed in the opening sentence of the **12–002** note: and *The Queen (on the application of Mohammed) v The Secretary of State for the Home Department* [2014] EWHC 1898 (Admin).

NOTE 8: Add at the end of the note: A further case is *Bostridge v Oxleas NHS Foundation Trust* [2015] EWCA Civ. 79, where the claimant was a mentally disordered patient and the defendant an NHS trust, which had detained the patient unlawfully, rather than the Secretary of State for the Home Department. In *Bostridge* the Court of Appeal held that for a nominal damages award it mattered not that it was not the NHS trust but a third party that could and would have lawfully detained the claimant.

Add at the end of the paragraph: In *Greer v Alstons Engineering Sales and* **12–005** *Services Ltd (Trinidad and Tobago)* [2003] UKPC 46, the Privy Council held that the appellants were entitled to a substantial award of damages for loss of use of a backhoe despite the failure of the appellants to prove any actual use of the backhoe. The Privy Council said that although "loss under this head was unquantified, it is the duty of the court to recognise it by an award that is not out of scale". However, the award of $5,000 was not disturbed because, although on the low side, it was not contrary to principle.

NOTE 23: Add at the end of the note: £5 as the award reappears in *The Queen* **12–006** *(on the application of Mohammed) v The Secretary of State for the Home Department* [2014] EWHC 1898 (Admin).

NOTE 34: Insert after "illustrative" on line two of the note: as is *Bostridge v* **12–009** *Oxleas NHS Foundation Trust* [2015] EWCA Civ. 79.

CHAPTER 13

EXEMPLARY DAMAGES

Add at the end of the paragraph: Exemplary damages have again been awarded **13–018** against immigration officers in *Patel v Secretary of State for the Home Department* [2014] EWHC 501 (Admin) (see *ibid.* at [343]) to a youngish Indian woman with leave to enter the United Kingdom to visit her family who was treated appallingly by the officers in their attempt to remove her from the country. See the case further at paras 40–015 and 40–025, below.

Insert a new note after the first sentence of the paragraph: **13–025**

NOTE 135a: Similar is the potential profit to be made by property owners harassing a neighbouring owner into giving up a right of way over their land, as in *Saxton v Bayliss* Unreported 31 January 2014 Central London County Court (facts at para.41–019 n.81, below).

CHAPTER 15

LIQUIDATED DAMAGES

15–008   Add at the end of the paragraph: In the important case of *Makdessi v Cavendish Square Holdings* [2013] EWCA Civ. 1539 Christopher Clarke LJ, in the only reasoned judgment in the Court of Appeal, conducted a most extensive review of the law and authorities on liquidated damages and penalties: see *ibid.* at [44]–[104]. For details of the case, see paras 15–012A to 15–012I, below.

Insert new paragraphs after para.15–012:

15–012A   The important case of *Makdessi v Cavendish Square Holdings* [2013] EWCA Civ. 1539 introduces us to penalties arising from provisions disentitling the party in breach from receiving sums of money which without breach he would have received and also deals with penalties arising from provisions requiring the transfer of property by the party in breach at an undervalue or for no value. This latter type of provision has already been addressed in a consideration of *Jobson v Johnson* [1989] 1 W.L.R. 1026 CA, see para.15–012.

15–012B   The *Makdessi* case is factually complicated. Mr Makdessi, a key figure in the advertising and marketing communications field in the Middle East, founded a group of companies operating in that field. The shares in the holding company of the group were held in near equal proportions by Mr Makdessi and a colleague, with a slight preponderance in favour of Mr Makdessi and with a little over 10 per cent of the shares held by a related company. Mr Makdessi and his colleague contracted to sell such of their shares to the related company as to give it a 60 per cent holding, which then became the holding of Cavendish Square Holdings on its substitution by novation agreement as a party to the contract. The purchase price was to be paid in instalments, described in order of due payment as the completion, the second, the interim and the final payments. The completion and second of these were fixed payments amounting together to just over $65 million but the interim and final payments could only be calculated in the future, being dependent on the amount of the company's future profits substantially increased to represent a particularly high figure for goodwill so that the total amount payable could amount to just short of $150 million. Two further provisions of importance appear in the contract. The sellers are given a put option whereby the purchaser can be required to buy the shares still held by them at a price reflecting the substantial increase made for goodwill to the company's future profits. The sellers enter into a covenant restricting them from trading in the same field in 23 specified countries.

15–012C   A clause in the contract provided in a sub-clause that, if either of the sellers were in breach of the restriction against trading, the purchasers would have an option to purchase the shares in the company still held by the defaulting seller at their net asset value with no increase on account of the high figure used for goodwill. Upon Mr Makdessi's breach of the trading restriction, Cavendish sought specific performance of the call option for his shares.

The same clause in the contract provided in a further sub-clause that, if either of the sellers were in breach of the restriction against trading, the seller in breach would cease to be entitled to the interim and final payments. Upon Mr Makdessi's breach of the trading restriction, which came after his receipt of the completion and second payments, Cavendish declined to make the interim and final payments to him. **15–012D**

To the provision for the withholding of moneys that would otherwise be due to the party in breach, the Court of Appeal accepted that the law of penalties applied. Indeed Christopher Clarke LJ in his judgment stated that it was common ground that clauses of this kind today engaged the law of penalties, citing for this result the decisions in *Gilbert Ash (Northern) Ltd v Modern Engineering (Bristol) Ltd* [1974] A.C. 689 and *Firma C-Trade SA v Newcastle Protection & Indemnity Association* [1989] 1 Lloyd's Rep. 239 CA: see [2013] EWCA Civ. 1539 at [46]–[47]. Yet neither of these cases has in the past featured in discussions of the law on liquidated damages and penalties and, while there is some mention of penalties in both cases, it is doubted that they can be said to establish that the law of penalties applies to provisions disentitling contract breakers to the receipt of moneys otherwise owed to them. But be that as it may, it is clear that this is the position after the *Makdessi* decision. **15–012E**

To the provision for the transfer of property to the purchasers by the seller in breach, the Court of Appeal accepted that the law of penalties applied. In so doing, the court was following *Jobson v Johnson* [1989] 1 W.L.R. 1026 CA (referred to at para.15–012A, above; the citation of the case in the judgment with its reference to 2 W.L.R. is wrong). **15–012F**

The Court of Appeal went on to decide that the provision for withholding moneys was indeed penal insofar as it could not be regarded as a genuine pre-estimate of Cavendish's loss. When the contract was made the sums that might be withheld were undetermined which militated against the provision for withholding being a genuine pre-estimate; the non-payment to Mr Maldessi could be of the bulk of his share of the purchase price since he stood to lose up to some $44 million and it was likely that his loss would be in millions or tens of millions of dollars; a trifling breach or one that was short-lived would have the same effect as one of substantial gravity: see the discussion at *ibid.* at [107]–[113]. **15–012G**

The Court of Appeal went on to decide that Cavendish's exercise of the call option for Mr Makdessi's shares was indeed penal insofar as it too could not be regarded as a genuine pre-estimate of Cavendish's loss. As was said in the judgment, similar considerations apply as with the provision for the withholding **15–012H** of moneys. Thus any loss that Cavendish would incur was indeterminate at the time of contract, the exercise of the call option and the consequent inability to exercise the put option could lead to a loss to Mr Makdessi amounting to tens of millions of dollars, and a trifling or short-lived breach would bring the breach provision into play: see the discussion at [2013] EWCA Civ. 1539 at [114]–[116].

15–012I   Holding neither provision to be a genuine pre-estimate of loss was not, however, the end of the day. It, said Christopher Clarke LJ, was not conclusive as showing a commercial justification for the provisions might mean that, though not genuine pre-estimates, they were not penal: *ibid.* at [117]. This is thought to be a somewhat novel approach to the resolution of the issue between liquidated damages and penalty. While commercial considerations have always been taken into account—in *Dunlop v Pneumatic Tyre Co v New Garage and Motor Co* [1915] A.C. 79 introducing for penalties the traditional terminology of a provision *in terrorem* commercial considerations were taken into account and in *Lordsvale Finance Plc v Bank of Zambia* [1996] Q.B. 752 introducing the revised terminology of a provision intended to deter breach there is a reference to commercial justification (for the old and the new terminology see, respectively, para.15–014 and para.15–018, below)—this appeared to be to assist in coming to a view of whether there is a genuine pre-estimate of loss within the wide meaning given to that term. However, the new approach, which is an eminently sensible one, seems to be here to stay: see the *Edgeworth* case immediately following at paras 15–012J to 15–012L. In *Makdessi* itself the Court of Appeal found no commercial justification for either of the provisions. See the whole discussion at [2013] EWCA Civ. 1539 at [118]–[125].

15–012J   The Supreme Court has now heard an appeal from the decision of the Court of Appeal in *Makdessi*. In addition to those issues considered by the Court of Appeal, on 21-23 July 2015, the Supreme Court considered whether the rule against penalties should be abolished in circumstances where sophisticated parties enter a commercial contract.

15–012K   *Edgeworth Capital (Luxembourg) SARL v Ramblas Investments BV* [2015] EWHC 150 (Comm) returns us to the question of whether a sum payable in circumstances other than a contractual breach can be a penalty. The facts of the case are far too complicated to allow for a summary here and the report of Hamblen J's decision needs to be consulted for this. In issue was whether a fee of some €100 million due under an agreement was a penalty. The agreement was part of a series of financing agreements entered into in relation to the purchase of a sizable property for the headquarters of a leading Spanish bank. The fee was to be paid in various tranches, payments being advanced in certain events which were not triggered by contractual breaches.

15–012L   Hamblen J noted, *ibid.* at [59], that the rule that penalty provisions only apply in the event of a breach of contract has been criticised on the grounds that it may lead to the rule being avoided by skilful drafting and that it may place a party terminating a contract under a contractual right in a worse position than a party breaking a contract. There was little doubt, he added, that this rule represents the law, citing the high authority of *Export Credits Guarantee Department v Universal Oil Products Co* [1983] 1 W.L.R. 399 HL (see para.15–009, below). Accordingly, he held the provision not to be a penalty, relying also on the fact that the provision did not require a larger payment but only an advanced payment: [2015] EWHC 150 at [67]–[70].

15–012M

At the same time Hamblen J held that, if it could be said that the fee was somehow to be treated as having been triggered by a breach of contract, there were grounds for considering that the amount of the fee was not a genuine pre-estimate of loss. Nevertheless, on this basis he would have held that, even though the fee were not a genuine pre-estimate of loss, the provision was commercially justifiable and its predominant function was not deterrence: at [71]–[73]. Therefore the fee was payable.

Insert a new note at the end of the paragraph:

15–013

NOTE 50a: Recent authorities, however, indicate that, even if the stipulated sum is not a genuine pre-estimate of loss, it will not be regarded as a penalty if there is a commercial justification for it: see the *Makdessi* and *Edgeworth* cases as referred to at paras 15–012I and 15–012L, above.

Insert a new paragraph after para.15–021:

The circumstances in which the rules about contractual penalties are invoked were novel in *ParkingEye Ltd v Beavis* [2015] EWCA Civ. 402. The claimant company managed a car park intended for motorist customers of a retail store. A parking charge of £85 was imposed on motorists for overstaying the two-hour permitted period of free parking, and motorists by parking were considered to have contracted to adhere to the parking rules. The defendant motorist overstayed the free period by just short of an hour and declined to pay the £85 charge, maintaining that it was a penalty. By the conventional standard of assessment of contractual penalties this was undoubtedly true. The overstaying charge was intended to deter from breach and was in no way a genuine pre-estimate of loss, there being indeed no loss at all to the claimant company. Despite this, the Court of Appeal sensibly held the overstaying charge to be enforceable. It was pointed out that the cases in the books have been of contracts of a financial and economic nature where the transaction can be assessed in monetary terms making the conventional penalty test appropriate. By contrast, the penalty test was inappropriate for a contract in which financial and economic considerations were of no relevance. Accordingly, the court concentrated upon whether the parking charge provision was extravagant and unconscionable in amount, a test also appearing in the early House of Lords cases (see para.15–032, below), and held

15–021A

that it was not. It was therefore enforceable. Just as today courts have begun to implement what would otherwise be regarded as unenforceable penalties if there is a commercial justification for them (see para.15–012I, above), so here a justification for the parking charge provision was found in more social factors.

15–022   Insert a new note at the end of the paragraph:

NOTE 76A: However, as pointed out by Leggatt J in *MSC Mediterranean Shipping Co SA v Cottonex Anstalt* [2015] EWHC 283 (Comm), in assessing whether a stipulated sum is or is not a penalty, the mitigation principle must be taken into account in comparing with the stipulated sum what the claimant would have recovered in the absence of the stipulated sum: *ibid.* at [113].

15–023   NOTE 77: Add at the end of the note: The *Bath* case was applied in *AB v CD* [2014] EWCA Civ. 229. At [30], Underhill LJ (with whom Ryder and Laws LJJ agreed) said that a claimant will still need to show that if the threatened breach occurs then there is a substantial risk of unrecoverable loss due to the liquidated damages provision. But once this is shown there will be a discretion to award an injunction. Ryder LJ would have gone further and seen this as one factor in a test for whether it is "just in all the circumstances" to confine a claimant to damages (at [32]).

Insert new paragraphs after para.15–030:

15–030A   An unusual situation arose in *MSC Mediterranean Shipping Co SA v Cottonex Anstalt* [2015] EWHC 283 (Comm) with a provision that was undoubtedly one for liquidated damages at the time when the contract was made becoming a penalty in the course of time. The Swiss seller of a large consignment of raw cotton to a purchaser in Bangladesh, both being companies, contracted to have it shipped by a carrier in 35 of the carrier's sea containers. The contract of carriage provided that for 14 days after the discharge of the cargo in the containers the shipper was entitled to retain the containers without charge, after which time what is today referred to as container demurrage (see para.15–073, below) at a specified daily rate was payable until the containers were returned, a provision that was completely open-ended so that payment of demurrage could continue indefinitely.

15–030B   The market for raw cotton having collapsed shortly after the conclusion of the contract of sale, the purchaser sought to extricate itself from the contract and did not collect the cotton which remained in the containers up to the time of the trial. The purchaser attempted not to make payment to the seller but its attempt, by resort to litigation, failed and payment was eventually made. On payment, title passed out of the seller who then had no control over the containers still with the cotton in them.

Leggatt J held that, once the seller was in repudiatory breach of contract, the **15–030C** carrier was obliged to accept the breach, thereby bringing the demurrage provision to an end, since it had no legitimate interest in not doing so; this aspect of the case is dealt with at paras 9–030A to 9–030E, above. Had he not so held, he would have held the demurrage provision a penalty, with the same result. This was because, even if the carrier had, in Leggatt J's words, an unfettered right not to accept the repudiatory breach, it was impossible to justify on compensatory grounds a provision which, even if there was no continuing loss to the carrier, it was entitled to recover demurrage indefinitely: see the whole discussion from *ibid.* at [94] onwards.

Insert in the text after the second sentence of the paragraph: Stipulated sums **15–073** payable to carriers of goods in their shipping containers, graduated to the length of time after they should have been returned to the carrier, have today come to be classified as demurrage, specifically as container demurrage. *MSC Mediterranean Shipping Co SA v Cottonex Anstalt* [2015] EWHC 283 (Comm), discussed at paras 9–030A to 9–030E and paras 15–030A to 15–030C, above, is such a case, and probably the first such case: see *ibid.* at [38].

CHAPTER 16

VINDICATORY DAMAGES

Insert a new note after "actionable *per se*" on the last line but four of the   **16–014**
paragraph:

NOTE 50a: The Court of Appeal in *Bostridge v Oxleas NHS Foundation Trust*
[2015] EWCA Civ. 79 held that where, unlike the defendant Secretary of State
for the Home Department in *Lumba*, the defendant NHS trust had no power
lawfully to detain the claimant, a mentally disordered patient, but he could and
would have been lawfully detained anyway by a third party, there was still an
entitlement only to nominal damages as there was no loss. Delivering the only
reasoned judgment in the Court of Appeal, Vos LJ recorded that the appellant's
counsel had disavowed any argument based upon the Earl of Halsbury's famous
dictum in *The Mediana* [1900] AC 113 at 117, discussed at para.35–044,
below.

BOOK THREE

VARIOUS GENERAL FACTORS IN THE ASSESSMENT OF DAMAGES

THE AWARDING OF INTEREST

NOTE 389: Add at the end of the note: *Network Rail Infrastructure Ltd v* **18–098**
Hardy [2015] EWHC1460 (TTC) is a case other than of personal injury where
delay, which was pleaded, was held not to cut down the interest award. The
earlier judgment on the damages to be awarded is at para.37–028, below.

18–121   NOTE 553: Add at the end of the note: The claim for interest was in US dollars in *Somasteel SARL v Coresteel DMCC* Unreported 20 April 2015, an action for non-delivery of goods sold, but, since the buyer's interests were in Morocco and its financial interests arose in Morocco, interest was awarded at the historical Moroccan rate.

BOOK FOUR

PARTICULAR CONTRACTS AND TORTS

BOOK FOUR

PART ONE

CONTRACT

CHAPTER 23

SALE OF GOODS

Insert a new note at the end of the paragraph: **23–003**

NOTE 4a: The loss of profits claim for breach by non-delivery under the first of two contracts for the sale of steel billets in *Somasteel SARL v Coresteel DMCC* Unreported 29 April 2015, got nowhere as there was held to be an available market. Therefore s.51(3) applied.

NOTE 11: Add at the end of the note: Nominal damages were awarded for **23–004** breach by non-delivery under the second of two contracts for the sale of steel billets in *Somasteel SARL v Coresteel DMCC* Unreported 29 April 2015, as the market price had fallen well below the contract price.

NOTE 48: Add at the end of the note: Interestingly, in *Somasteel SARL v* **23–014** *Coresteel DMCC* Unreported 29 April 2015, an action for non-delivery of goods sold where there was held to be an available market, the trial judge arrived at a market price not by concentrating on the buyer's actions, as the cases preceding above do, but by taking the average price based on similar contracts that the seller had made around the time of the contract.

23–023   Insert a new note at the end of the paragraph:

NOTE 105a: One item of recovery in the complex damages case of *Thai Airways International Public Co Ltd v KI Holdings Co Ltd* [2015] EWHC 1250 (Comm), where there was non-delivery of a number of economy class seats sold for installation in aircraft, was the additional cost of purchasing of replacement seats, subject to certain credits. See at *ibid.* at [20] with [141] et seq., and the case in detail at para.9–006A, above.

23–044   Insert a new note at the end of the paragraph:

NOTE 189a: One item of recovery in the complex damages case of *Thai Airways International Public Co Ltd v KI Holdings Co Ltd* [2015] EWHC 1250 (Comm), where there was delayed delivery of a number of economy class seats sold for installation in aircraft, was the additional cost of purchasing, before delivery had taken place, of replacement seats, subject to certain credits. See *ibid.* at [18], [19] with [141] et seq., and the case in detail at para.9–006A, above.

23–060   Insert a new note at the end of the paragraph:

NOTE 254a: A buyer is entitled to recover for consequential losses arising from the breach of warranty on top of recovery for the normal measure. The arbitration award was therefore held to be wrong in *Saipol SA v Inerco Trade SA* [2014] EWHC 2211 (Comm) as it had limited the buyer of sunflower seed oil, contaminated in the shipping of it, to the normal measure by applying s.53(3) instead of s.53(2).

23–086   Insert a new note at the end of the paragraph:

NOTE 373a: The Court of Appeal in *Stacey v Autosleeper Group Ltd* [2014] EWCA Civ. 1551 (facts in note to para.8–147, above) endorsed the trial judge's allowing recovery of costs paid to the third party, but not in full as they had been increased by the buyer's unreasonable conduct: *ibid.* at [24], [25].

CHAPTER 27

SALE OF SHARES AND LOAN OF STOCK

Add at the end of the first sentence of the paragraph: This is confirmed and **27–008** applied in all of three cases in the circumstances of which it was held that events subsequent to the breach were not to be taken into account. These are *Ageas (UK) Ltd v Kwik-Fit (GB) Ltd* [2014] EWHC 2178 QB, *Hut Group Ltd v Nobahar-Cookson* [2014] EWHC 3842 QB and *Bir Holdings Ltd v Mehta* [2014] EWHC 3903 Ch, considered in detail at para.10–120, above.

CHAPTER 30

CONTRACTS OF CARRIAGE

Insert a new paragraph after para.30–075:

In *Louis Dreyfus Commodities Suisse SA v MT Maritime Management BV,* **30–075A**
"MTM Hong Kong" [2015] EWHC 2505 (Comm) Males J considered whether
damages should be restricted to the losses suffered up until the point when the
contract voyage would have come to an end. The charterers submitted that *Smith
v McGuire* (1858) 3 H & N 554 permitted only the recovery of losses until the
point that the contract voyage had ended, although there was no claim in that case
for losses beyond the point when the contract voyage had ended. The difference
was substantial. The *Smith v McGuire* (1858) 3 H & N 554 measure would have
led to an award in favour of the shipowner of US$478,386. The amount which
was awarded by the arbitral tribunal resulted in an award of almost three times
this amount.

The reason for the difference was that additional consequential loss was
suffered by the owners because performance of the contract voyage would not
only have enabled the owners to earn the freight payable under the voyage

charter but it would also have ensured that the vessel was situated in Europe without delay at the conclusion of the voyage, ready to take advantage of the higher freights available in the North Atlantic market. The charterers' repudiation meant that the owners had to mitigate by taking a different charter, which delayed the repositioning of the vessel causing the loss of two lucrative transatlantic charters that could have been performed in the same time as the mitigation charter. The primary judge upheld the arbitral tribunal's award of these consequential losses.

CHAPTER 31

CONTRACTS OF EMPLOYMENT

NOTE 54: Add at the end of the note: *Lavarack* and *Horkulak* come under discussion in *IBM United Kingdom Holdings Ltd v Dalgleish* [2015] EWHC 389 Ch where there was not wrongful dismissal but breach of the duty of trust and confidence. See the case at para.31–031 n.185a, below.

31–011

Insert a new note at the end of the paragraph:

31–031

NOTE 185a: Breach of the obligation of trust and confidence again features in *IBM United Kingdom Holdings Ltd v Dalgleish* [2015] EWHC 389 Ch, which involved an employer's scheme to vary the contractual rights of employees by making their salaries non-pensionable in return for salary increases. Warren J's judgment is concerned with the entitlement to damages rather than with their assessment but there is much discussion on damages (*ibid.* at [139]–[178]). See the references to the case at paras.10–111 n.494 and 31–011 n.54, above.

Add at the end of the paragraph: In *Merlin Financial Consultants v Cooper* [2015] EWHC 1196 QB, where the employee was in breach of a restrictive covenant by setting up a competing business on the termination of his employment, the employer was awarded damages based on the profits that it would have made from the clients who had left, subject to a deduction, as an expense, of the amount payable to a replacement employee, and subject in addition to a percentage deduction from these profits as the trial judge was of the view that some of the clients would have left anyway, even if the employee had not been in breach of his contractual obligations: see *ibid.* at [74]–[83].

31–040

BOOK FOUR

PART TWO

TORT

TORTS AFFECTING GOODS: DAMAGE AND DESTRUCTION

Insert a new paragraph after para.35–024:

There being a whole range of basic hire rates offered on the market for **35–024A** vehicles generally and therefore for vehicles of the type that it was reasonable for the particular claimant to hire, judges at the lower level have had much difficulty in deciding on the basic hire rate appropriate in the case before them. The Court of Appeal in *Stevens v Equity Syndicate Management Ltd* [2015] EWCA Civ. 93 has now given guidance. The claimant there had entered into a credit hire agreement but, being held not to be impecunious, was entitled to claim only the basic hire rate. Accordingly, the Court of Appeal started by considering how the basic hire element in the total charged under the credit hire agreement was to be ascertained. It proving impractical to find this out as it would require disclosure and analysis at a cost in excess of the value of the claim, the court resorted to looking at basic hire rates available in the claimant's locality, which is what the lower courts in the case had attempted to do: *ibid.* at [30]–[32]. If, as is likely, there is a range of rates, the court must seek out the lowest reasonable rate quoted by a mainstream supplier, or in the absence of a mainstream supplier by a local reputable supplier, for a vehicle of the kind in issue to a reasonable person in the position of the claimant: *ibid.* at [32]–[40]. Kitchin LJ's judgment, the only reasoned one given, reviews the major authorities and merits study.

35–025   Add at the end of the paragraph: The Court of Appeal has now made it crystal clear in *Zurich Insurance Plc v Sameer* [2014] EWCA Civ. 357 that a claimant's entitlement to rely on impecuniosity goes to the duration of hire as much as to the rate of hire. Impecuniosity could justify a higher level of award where the claimant continued to hire due to inability to pay for repairs or to buy a replacement car: *ibid.* at [9(4)]. The case itself was concerned only with the interpretation of an order debarring the claimant, whose car was a write-off, from relying on his impecuniosity and with whether the order covered the duration of hiring as well as the rate of hire. A further issue mentioned but not argued was whether the rules of mitigation required the claimant to claim on his insurance policy and with the proceeds buy a replacement car; the court said that, while this was an interesting question of some importance, it was for another day: *ibid.* at [41]–[43].

35–059   The words "based on te capital" should be "based on the capital".

NOTE 305: Add at the end of the note: See also *Bee v Jenson* [2007] EWCA Civ 923.

TORTS AFFECTING LAND

Add at the end of the paragraph: **37–028**

In *Network Rail Infrastructure Ltd v Handy* [2015] EWHC 1175 (TTC), Akenhead J described the proceedings as involving a sense of "déjà vu". Again, when the defendants damaged the railway track in this case several different points were raised that had not been previously raised, or had been conceded. Again, the defendants were found to be liable to pay damages for the losses suffered by Network Rail under the agreed formula.

One argument made by the defendants was that the imposition of damages based on a formula that was agreed between the claimant a third parties could be unreasonable. Akenhead J, following comments in the Court of Appeal in the *Conarken Group* case, explained that there is no overarching or separate principle that requires damages to be reasonable as between claimant and defendant.

However, if the amount of agreed damages were extremely large, then even if those damages had been suffered they might be reduced based on principles of causation, remoteness, mitigation, or a focus on the scope of the tortious duty.

Another issue was whether economic loss was recoverable in a trespass action when there was no physical damage to land. It was held that neither in negligence nor in trespass was physical damage necessary. In negligence cases it is sufficient if the breach of duty results in substances or physical things being deposited on the property in question in more than a de minimis manner such that the property cannot be used or enjoyed as it otherwise would or could be if the substances or physical things had not been so deposited. In trespass cases, economic losses can be recovered even if there is no damage to, or fouling of, the land. An example given was a defendant who trespasses by parking a fleet of lorries on the claimant's land. Even if there is no physical damage to the land a reasonable charge could be recovered based on the income the claimant land-owner might reasonably have charged for lorries to park there. This would be equivalent to a loss of income.

CHAPTER 38

TORTS CAUSING PERSONAL INJURY

[65]

38–001   NOTE 1: Add at the end of the note: In any event the existence of physical or psychiatric injury has to be clearly established. This could not be done with sensitisation from exposure at work to platinum salts in *Greenway v Johnson Matthey Plc* [2014] EWHC 3957 QB (see *ibid.* at [13] et seq. and the facts at para.8–134, above) any more than with the pleural plaques in *Rothwell v Chemical and Insulating Co* [2008] A.C. 281 (at para.5–012, above). See also the decision of the same judge (Jay J) in *Saunderson v Sonae Industria (UK) Ltd* [2015] EWHC 2264 QB at [178].

38–005   NOTE 16: Add at the end of the note: Where with liability admitted the court is satisfied that substantial damages will be awarded but it is currently difficult to conclude accurately what sum will be recovered, the assessment must be carried out on a conservative basis and the risk of overpayment avoided: *AS v West Suffolk Hospital Trust* Unreported (as yet) 1 May 2015.

38–040   Insert a new note at the end of the paragraph:

NOTE 128a: For a different approach to consecutive injuries, see *Reaney v University Hospital of North Staffordshire NHS Trust* [2014] EWHC 3016 QB at para.8–090 n.448, above.

Insert a new paragraph after para.38–099:

38–099A   The discussion in the immediately preceding paragraph supporting the survival of *Smith v Manchester* is also supported by the Explanatory Notes made by the Ogden Working Party that there will be circumstances in which the *Smith v Manchester* approach would still be appropriate. One of those circumstances arose in *Billett v Ministry of Defence* [2015] EWCA Civ 773. There, the claimant had suffered an injury to his feet whilst serving in the army. The trial judge had made an award of £99,062.04 based upon the Ogden Tables for loss of earning capacity. The Court of Appeal held that the Ogden Tables should not have been applied because there was no evidence of how the claimant would be classified within a scale of degree of impairment and if the Ogden Tables were applied without adjustment the award for future loss of earning capacity would be hopelessly unrealistic for the claimant who was pursuing his chosen career as a lorry driver without hindrance. The exercise of making an adjustment to the reduction factors in the Ogden Tables would be no more scientific than the broad brush judgment that the court makes when taking the *Smith v Manchester* approach. It was preferable to apply *Smith v Manchester* because: (i) the claimant was at the very margins of the definition of disability; (ii) his disability affected his activities outside work much more than it affected his work; and (iii) there was no rational basis for determining how the reduction factor should be adjusted. Applying *Smith v Manchester*, the Court of Appeal awarded an amount of £45,000 for the future earning capacity in place of the trial judge's award of £99,062.04.

Insert a new note at the end of the paragraph: **38–112**

NOTE 508a: In *Totham v King's College Hospital NHS Foundation Trust* [2015] EWHC 97 QB the trial judge also wished to see the *Croke* decision overruled as she agreed with the Court of Appeal's criticisms of it in *Iqbal*, which criticisms, as stated in this work, are thought to be misconceived.

Add at the end of the paragraph: In some cases the Ogden criteria might not **38–137** be applied at all. These cases will be where the degree of disability is very small, the effect upon a claimant's work is not significant, and there is no rational basis for determining how the reduction factor should be adjusted: *Billett v Ministry of Defence* [2015] EWCA Civ 773, discussed above at para.38–099A.

Insert a new paragraph after para.38–186:

The passage into law of the Care Act 2014 has not altered these principles, **38–186A** although s.22 of that Act provides that the duties and powers to meet a person's needs for care and support are now qualified because, with limited exceptions, a local authority may not meet those needs by providing or arranging for the provision of a service or facility that is required to be provided under the National Health Service Act.

Add at the end of the paragraph: In *Ellison v University Hospitals of Mor-* **38–196** *ecambe Bay NHS Foundation Trust* [2015] EWHC 366 QB the very substantial cost of installing and maintaining an in-home hydrotherapy pool was held justified as an item in the damages awarded since use of the pool was the one way of relieving the excessive pain suffered by the severely disabled child claimant: see the lengthy passage in the judgment at *ibid.* at [78]–[120].

NOTE 902: Add at the end of the note: In *Ellison v University Hospitals of* **38–198** *Morecambe Bay NHS Foundation Trust* [2015] EWHC 366 QB Warby J relied on Swift J's reasoning and judgment so as to hold, as with her, that there should be no deduction on account of any benefit to the child's parents from living free in the house suitable for the disabled child which was to be acquired; it was the child's claim and any such deduction would bring down the damages so as to leave the child under-compensated: see the passage in his judgment, which analyses other cases dealing with the issue, *ibid.* at [134]–[152].

38–216   Add at the end of the paragraph: In *Manna (A Child) v Central Manchester University Hospitals NHS Foundation Trust* [2015] EWHC 2279 QB, Cox J applied Table 28, recognising (at [185]) that the application of Table 1 would cause a double discount.

38–230   NOTE 1066: Add at the end of the note: *Evans* was applied in *FM v Ipswich Hospital NHS Trust* [2015] EWHC 775 QB, giving a discount of 25 per cent in preference to the defendant's proposal of a one third discount.

38–231   Insert a new note at the end of the paragraph:

NOTE 1079a: Where in *Totham v King's College Hospital NHS Foundation Trust* [2015] EWHC 97 QB a mother had given up a well-paid job to care for her daughter brain damaged at birth, the trial judge's award of only the commercial rate discounted in the usual way is surely wrong: see *ibid.* at [23]–[28].

CHAPTER 39

TORTS CAUSING DEATH

39–029   NOTE 159: Add at the end of the note: See for a high percentage chance, at 80 per cent, *Hayes v South East Coast Ambulance Service NHS Foundation Trust* [2015] EWHC 18 QB (divorced couple had come together again even with talk of remarriage: *ibid.* at [146]–[149]).

39–083   NOTE 403: Insert at the beginning of the note: Cost of carers and a variety of other costs not agreed by the parties to the action were awarded in *Zambarda v Shipbreaking (Queensborough) Ltd* [2013] EWHC 2263 QB.

39–125   Insert a new note before "Exceptionally" on line four of the paragraph:

NOTE 630a: A variety of costs were awarded in the estate action in *Zambarda v Shipbreaking (Queensborough) Ltd* [2013] EWHC 2263 QB.

39–126   Insert in the text after the indented citation from Parker LJ in the middle of the paragraph: For rather different reasons, the Court of Appeal in *Kadir v Mistry* [2014] EWCA Civ. 1177 agreed with the trial judge's refusal to award any damages for pain and suffering. Diagnosis of cancer in the deceased had been negligently delayed. Had there been no delay the deceased would have suffered the same symptoms, although somewhat later and in the interim would have been subjected to painful treatment to deal with the cancer. Laws LJ, giving the only reasoned judgment, stressed that there were no special rules for assessing pain and suffering in estate claims; the criterion is, as always, to put the now deceased in the same position as he or she would have been if the negligence had not occurred: *ibid.* at [11], [12].

39–127   Add at the end of the paragraph: We have seen (at para.38–259, above) that, while awards of damages for loss of expectation of life have been abolished, damages for pain and suffering may take into account suffering caused by awareness that expectation of life has been reduced. The Court of Appeal in *Kadir v Mistry* [2014] EWCA Civ. 1177 (facts at para.39–126, above) differed from the trial judge and awarded damages for mental suffering on account of the deceased's belief that, had her cancer been diagnosed earlier, she would have had a chance of survival. The case is perhaps particular in that there was an award for mental distress at the contemplation of a reduced life span with no award for pain and suffering independently of this element.

CHAPTER 40

ASSAULT AND FALSE IMPRISONMENT

Insert a new paragraph after para.40–007:

The same approach which recognises a substantial award of aggravated dam-   **40–007A**
ages can be seen in *Mohidin v Commissioner of Police of the Metropolis* [2015]
EWHC 2740 QB. In that case, one of the claimants was held to have been falsely
imprisoned and assaulted by the police. His award for false imprisonment was
£4,500 and, for the minor assault, £250. However, to these basic awards was
added aggravated damages of £7,200 for the racially abusive and intimidating
way in which the assault and false imprisonment was committed.

Add at the end of the paragraph: On the other hand, in *Patel v Secretary of*   **40–015**
State for the Home Department [2014] EWHC 501 (Admin) the seriousness of
the misconduct of immigration officers, where the false imprisonment was for the
comparatively short period of six days, was held to justify an award of £20,000,
even before aggravated damages and exemplary damages (for which, see paras
40–023 and 40–025, below) were brought in. The case was considered under the
Human Rights Act as well as under the common law of false imprisonment, the
breaches of Human Rights Act articles adding significantly to the damages
award: see *ibid.* at [330], [336]–[342]. As for the unlawful detention for 61 days
of an unaccompanied asylum-seeking young person, this led in *AS v Secretary of*
State for the Home Department [2015] EWHC 1331 QB to an award of £23,000,
before aggravated damages were brought in (for which, see para.40–023,
below).

NOTE 95: Add at the end of the note: A further such case is *The Queen (on*   **40–018**
the application of Mohammed) v The Secretary of State for the Home Department
[2014] EWHC 1898 (Admin). A different type of case in which only nominal

damages were awarded for a false imprisonment is *Bostridge v Oxleas NHS Foundation Trust* [2015] EWCA Civ. 79 where a mentally disordered patient had been unlawfully detained by an NHS trust.

40–019   Add at the end of the paragraph: There was an additional award for psychiatric illness in *AS v Secretary of State for the Home Department* [2015] EWHC 1331 QB (facts at para.40–015, above).

40–023   Add at the end of the paragraph: Aggravated damages of £5,000 were awarded in *AS v Secretary of State for the Home Department* [2015] EWHC 1331 QB where an unaccompanied asylum-seeking young person was unlawfully detained for 61 days. The aggravating features recognised by the trial judge are detailed at *ibid.* at [13]. Aggravated damages of £30,000 were awarded in *Patel v Secretary of State for the Home Department* [2014] EWHC 501 (Admin), with the aggravating factors summarised at *ibid.* at [332]; see the case at para.40–015, above. And aggravated damages of £2,300 (claimant 1) and £7,200 (claimant 2) were awarded in *Mohidin v Commissioner of Police of the Metropolis* [2015] EWHC 2740 QB, where false imprisonment and assault by police officers was accompanied by racial abuse and humiliation.

40–024   NOTE 134: Add at the end of the note: Separate awards continue to be made, as in *AS v Secretary of State for the Home Department* [2015] EWHC 1331 QB and in *Patel v Secretary of State for the Home Department* [2014] EWHC 501 (Admin): see paras 40–015 and 40–023, above.

40–025   Add at the end of the paragraph: Exemplary damages, in the amount of £15,000, have now been awarded for arbitrary and oppressive conduct of immigration officers in *Patel v Secretary of State for the Home Department* [2014] EWHC 501 (Admin); see *ibid.* at [343] and the case at para.40–015, above.

Chapter 41

STATUTORY TORTS: DISCRIMINATION AND HARASSMENT

41–006 NOTE 16: Add at the end of the note: Cases of discrimination heard in the Employment Tribunal do not attract the 10 per cent uplift in damages for non-pecuniary loss introduced by *Simmons v Castle* [2013] 1 W.L.R. 1239 CA. It was so held in *De Souza v Vinci Construction UK Ltd* March 2015 EAT, the reasons for bringing in this uplift (for which see para.51–044, below) having no application to the Employment Tribunal. See too para.5–003 n.4, above.

41–007 Add at the end of the paragraph: There has been an appeal, [2014] EWCA Civ. 91, and, as predicted, the Court of Appeal endorsed the reduction, commenting that there was no justification for a one-off offensive comment being placed in the middle band: *ibid.* at [59].

Insert a new paragraph after para.41–014:

41–014A The concerns of Underhill J are, however, highlighted by situations in which the award of aggravated damages is made for injury to feelings caused by discrimination and harassment where the basic award is made for a different tort such as assault or false imprisonment. In *Mohidin v Commissioner of Police of the Metropolis* [2015] EWHC 2740 QB, the two successful claimants sought basic and aggravated damages for false imprisonment and assault by police officers. Their claim for aggravated damages relied upon racial abuse and humiliation inflicted by the police officers. The basic awards for false imprisonment and assault were, for each claimant, £200 (false imprisonment, claimant 1) and £4,500 (false imprisonment, claimant 2). To these basic awards were added aggravated damages, calculated in accordance with the *Vento* principles for basic awards of discrimination, of £2,300 (claimant 1) and £7,200 (claimant 2).

41–019   NOTE 81: Add at the end of the note: The award in *Saxton v Bayliss* Unreported 31 January 2014 Central London County Court, for harassment of an old lady by her very unpleasant neighbours causing her profound distress, the neighbours mounting a prolonged and vicious campaign to get her out of her house and thereby eliminate her right of way over their property, was £25,000. It would have been even higher in the absence of an additional exemplary award of £10,000.

INVASION OF PRIVACY

45–001 Add at the end of the paragraph: Now the Court of Appeal in *Google Inc v Vidal-Hall* [2015] EWCA Civ. 311 has concluded that misuse of private information should be recognised as a tort (*ibid.* at [51]), being a civil wrong without any equitable characteristics (*ibid.* at [43]). It was so held there for the purposes of service out of the jurisdiction (*ibid.* at [51]) but should have general application. For the case in relation to breach of confidence and confidential information, see para.46–026, below.

45–008 NOTE 46: Add at the end of the note: As pointed out in para.51–044, below, the primary purpose behind the introduction of a 10 per cent uplift in damages for non-pecuniary loss was to compensate those funding their claims by a conditional fee agreement for their inability, on success, to recover the success fee from the defendant where the conditional fee agreement was entered into after the costs-amending legislation came into force on 1 April 2013. The judge's refusal of the uplift in the class action entitled *Gulati v MGN Ltd* [2015] EWHC 1482 Ch (facts at para.45–008A, below) was on account of success fees still being available to the several claimants (see *ibid.* at [165]). This can only be on the basis that the claimants' conditional fee agreements dated from before 1 April 2013. Yet that this was so does not appear anywhere in the overlong judgment delivered in late May 2015.

Insert a new paragraph after para.45–008:

45–008A The road to higher awards has led to dramatic increases in the class action entitled *Gulati v MGN Ltd* [2015] EWHC 1482 Ch. Eight claimants sued for invasion of their privacy which came about by the hacking of their phones by journalists who listened to their voicemails on a daily basis over several years and then reported on what they heard in very many articles addressed to the public. The awards made by Mann J started at £72,500 and moved through the £100,000s to a top award of £260,000. He recognised that he was awarding much higher sums than had any of the earlier cases, but pointed out that the scale of the invasions of privacy was far greater in the case before him, being more serious and more prolonged. What also led to these awards being out of line with previous awards was that Mann J was giving compensation for loss of dignity as well as for the more conventional injury to feelings (on which, see para.5–014A, above). Whether awards of this level, even in an exceptional case as this was, will be endorsed by the Court of Appeal may be in some doubt.

ECONOMIC TORTS

NOTE 147: Substitute "below" with "above".   **46–026**

Add at the end of the paragraph: However, in *Google Inc v Vidal-Hall* [2015] EWCA Civ. 311 the Court of Appeal was of the view, contrary to what is said in this paragraph in the main text, that *Kitechnology BV v Unicor GmbH Plast-maschinen* [1995] F.S.R. 765 CA, by which the Court of Appeal considered itself bound, established that an action for breach of confidence is not an action in tort. It can be argued that what was said to this effect was obiter as the Court of Appeal held that the case before it was not one of breach of confidence but one of misuse of private information, which it held to be indeed a tort: see the chapter dealing with invasion of privacy at para.45–001, above. The concepts of confidence and privacy were said not to be the same and protected different interests: *ibid.* at [21]; actions for breach of confidence and actions for misuse of private information were said to rest on different legal foundations: *ibid.* at [25].

NOTE 184: Add at the end of the note: In *Primary Group (UK) Ltd v Royal*   **46–031**
Bank of Scotland Plc [2014] EWHC 1082 Ch the same trial judge, Arnold J, approached the assessment of damages against a bank sued for breach of confidence by an insurance company in the same way as he had in the *Force*

India case (see [181] et seq. of a long judgment), but the breach of confidence was a contractual one.

46–054   Insert a new note before the "and" ending the third line of the paragraph:

NOTE 326a: Damages have also been measured by a licence fee where the number of lost sales has been too speculative and too open to inaccuracy to be a sound basis for calculation. This was done in *Kohler Mira Ltd v Bristan Group Ltd* [2014] EWHC 1931 (IPEC), which concerned infringement of design right in electric shower units.

46–057   Add at the end of the paragraph: Yet it was held in *Kohler Mira Ltd v Bristan Group Ltd* [2014] EWHC 1931 (IPEC) that the claimant who had established infringement of design right in electric shower units was in principle entitled to damages in relation to products unprotected by the design right infringed if the damage was caused by the infringement, was foreseeable, and was not excluded by public policy: see *ibid.* at [28] et seq.

46–064   Add at the end of the paragraph: In *Pendle Metalwares Ltd v Walter Page (Safeway's) Ltd* [2014] EWHC 1140 Ch, His Honour Judge Purle awarded additional damages on account of the flagrancy of the infringement but refused them in respect of benefit accruing by reason of the infringement: see *ibid.* at [46]–[52].

46–071   NOTE 399: Add at the end of the note: In *Kohler Mira Ltd v Bristan Group Ltd* [2014] EWHC 1931 (IPEC), which concerned infringement of design right in electric shower units, it was appreciated that moral prejudice referred to non-pecuniary loss. The 10 per cent uplift asked for on the award given for pecuniary loss was therefore refused as there was no non-pecuniary loss. Non-pecuniary loss, it was rightly said, was likely to arise only in very particular circumstances: *ibid.* at [60]